Short in stature, but outsize in personality, a young Corsican professional soldier called Napoleon Bonaparte rose in little more than thirty years to become absolute ruler of France and half of Europe. Who was this remarkable man? How could France, which had so recently shaken the world with its revolutionary upheavals, tolerate as its leader this self-seeking military and political genius? What were the needs that his autocratic but reforming style of government was able to satisfy?

Stephen Pratt has written an acute and compelling study of Napoleon, and the nation he adopted. Filled with fascinating insights into attitudes of the time, the book examines Napoleon's career from second lieutenant of artillery, through the unstable Jacobin Terror and the Directorate, the military conquests in Italy and Egypt which made him the darling of the republic, to the *coup de Brumaire* which opened his way to absolute power. It analyzes his methods, contrasts his dealings with contemporary figures inside and outside France, and shows how the very momentum of his triumphs contained the seeds of his eventual downfall and lonely exile. Over 80 pictures and maps, table of dates, further reading, index.

Napoleon

Stephen Pratt

WAYLAND PUBLISHERS LIMITED

More Wayland Kings and Queens

Frontispiece Napoleon Bonaparte crossing the Alps, by Jacques Louis David.

SBN 85340 389 9
Copyright © 1976 by Wayland (Publishers) Ltd,
49 Lansdowne Place, Hove, East Sussex
Printed in Great Britain by
Biddles Ltd, Guildford, Surrey

Contents

Above Napoleon as Lieutenant of Artillery in the Régiment de la Fère, aged seventeen.

1 The Young Corsican

IN 1769 CORSICA WAS THE SCENE of a desperate struggle. The island had been sold to the French by the Genoese in 1768, and since then the Corsicans had fought bitterly to regain their land.

One of the men killed in the fighting was called Napoleone, a member of a leading Corsican family, the Buona Partes. On 15th August, 1769, the year he died, a cousin was born who was named after this valiant fighter. He was Napoleon Bonaparte.

The year after he was born, Napoleon's father, Carlo, made peace with the French and was duly admitted to the French nobility. Thanks to this and to his parents' friendship with Marbeuf, the French Governor of Corsica, Napoleon received the best military education available to the sons of French noblemen. He went first to a church school at Autun, in France, for three months, largely to learn French (his native language was Italian). From there he moved to Brienne, one of twelve royal schools in France for the sons of nobles.

Finally, in 1784, he moved to the *Ecole Militaire* in Paris—the best military college in France. As a king's scholar Napoleon was looked down on by the sons of the great French nobles, who paid expensive fees. He never forgot the snobbery at Brienne, nor the insults he suffered from his fellow students at the *Ecole Militaire*.

Napoleon was an excellent student. His performance in the passing-out examinations was so good that in 1785, after only one year at the *Ecole Militaire,* he was commissioned into one of the smartest artillery regiments in France—the "Régiment de la Fère" at Valence. Between 1785 and 1788 at Valence and at the

"Europe now turns her eyes upon them [*the Corsicans*] and with astonishment sees them on the eve of emancipating themselves from a foreign yoke." *James Boswell in his* Account of Corsica, *1768.*

"I remained his classmate in mathematics, at which to my mind he was indubitably the best in the School." *Louis de Bourrienne, a schoolfellow at Brienne who remained a friend of Napoleon throughout his career.*

Right The storming of the Bastille on 14th July, 1789. This was the first major event of the French Revolution.

"Bonaparte was distinguished at Brienne by his complexion . . . his piercing and searching glance, by the tone of his conversation with his masters and comrades. There was always something acid in his remarks. He was by no means affectionate." *Louis de Bourrienne.*

artillery school of Auxonne, Lieutenant Bonaparte received professional and practical training which was to be of great significance in his future career.

Life for the officers of King Louis XVI's army was leisurely. Between 1786 and 1788 Napoleon spent three quarters of his time on leave, either in Paris or in Corsica. At home family affairs occupied most of his time, for his father had died in 1785, and although the second son, Napoleon seems always to have taken the role of head of the family.

In 1789, while he was training at the artillery school of Auxonne, the French Revolution broke out. From the beginning Napoleon went with the tide of revolution. In September 1789 he returned to Corsica and took the lead in rallying support for what was going on in France, where the National Assembly (the parliament of the Revolution) declared that Corsicans should have the full rights and liberties of French citizens.

In 1791, back in France, Napoleon became a

Left Napoleon as Lieutenant-Colonel of the First Battalion of Corsica, aged twenty-one.

Republican when he heard of King Louis' attempted flight, and when he was next in Corsica took the Republican side in the political strife which was developing there. The Buona Parte family led the Republicans, and Paoli, a one-time friend, opposed them. When war broke out between revolutionary France and England in 1793, Paoli was denounced as pro-English by Napoleon's younger brother Lucien. Civil war broke out. Paoli was victorious, the whole Buona Parte family was forced into exile in France, and Corsica came under English control.

From this point Napoleon severed his connection with Corsica. The war between France and Europe, begun in 1792, was entering a crucial phase. Large numbers of aristocratic French officers had fled abroad, so that there were many opportunities for young officers of the Republican army who had the ability and initiative to seize them. Napoleon had more than his share of both, and in 1793 his meteoric rise began.

> "My dear Mother, today, when time has calmed a little the first transports of my grief, I hasten to show you the gratitude your goodness inspires in me. Be consoled, dear Mother, circumstances demand it. We will redouble our care and thankfulness and be happy if by our obedience we can make good a little the boundless loss of a dearly loved husband."
> *Napoleon in a letter to his mother on hearing of his father's death.*

Above The meeting of the Estates General at Versailles, 5th May, 1789.

2 Revolution and War

IN 1789 THE ESTATES GENERAL OF FRANCE met at Versailles, for the first time since 1614. The Estates General was a sort of parliament consisting of representatives of the Three Estates (classes): the Clergy, the Nobility, and the Commons, or Third Estate.

Louis XVI's government was bankrupt, and the king was handicapped by very out-of-date financial and legal systems. The nobles paid hardly any taxes and had all the high positions in the Church, Army and Navy reserved for them. The middle classes, part of the Third Estate, were jealous of the privileges of the nobility, and the peasants paid the bulk of the taxes.

Left Louis XVI of France, who was overthrown by the French Revolution in 1792.

The Revolution began when the Third Estate at Versailles turned itself into a National Assembly and declared that it was going to change the whole system of government in France by drawing up a constitution. This was to be a set of rules regulating the powers of the king and his ministers, the rights and duties of assemblies and how they should be elected. The National Assembly also freed the peasants from their feudal dues and services to their lords.

Unfortunately Louis XVI, although he swore an oath to the constitution, was not loyal to it. His heart was with his brothers and some of the great nobles who had fled abroad and become *émigrés*. He hated the way in which the Assembly confiscated Church lands, and in defiance of the Pope took the Church under its control.

In June 1791 Louis and his family tried to flee abroad to join his wife's brother, the Emperor of Austria. They were halted at Varennes near the Eastern frontier, and brought back to Paris as prisoners. From this point the revolutionaries split into two groups: those who wanted to continue with a constitutional monarchy and those who wanted to establish a republic. (Napoleon, as we know, became a Republican.)

In April 1792 France declared war on Austria. Most revolutionary leaders believed that war would be a final test of the king's loyalty, and act as a sort of strong medicine to cure the nation of any illness remaining from the bad old days. In fact, the war did have a dramatic effect on the course of the Revolution. The immediate failure of the French armies, the invasion of France by Prussia and Austria and the King's undoubted treachery (he betrayed war plans to the Emperor of Austria) led to the violent overthrow of the monarchy on 10th August, 1792, when a huge mob attacked the royal palace of the Tuileries.

From now on a quarrel developed between two types of Republican—the Girondins and the Jacobins. The Girondins, although Republican, were moderate and

very reluctant to take violent measures to win the war. The Jacobins thought that in the great struggle against Europe (England, Holland, and Spain had joined Austria and Prussia), everything should be sacrificed to save France and the Revolution. By July 1793 the Jacobins were in control. They developed a reign of terror to impose their policies such as control of prices and wages, conscription for the armies and ruthless suppression of their opponents. Anyone suspected of being anti-patriotic was quickly sent to the new beheading machine, the guillotine, where both the king and queen met their deaths.

Above Louis XVI's last farewell to his family on the day of his execution, 21st January, 1793.

Above A view of the harbour of Toulon.

Soon there was civil war in many parts of France, where Girondin supporters raised rebellion against the Jacobin dictatorship. Now it was that Napoleon had his great chance. In the South the Girondins were in control of the great naval base of Toulon and had handed it over to the British fleet. The Jacobins sent an army to besiege the port. Napoleon, now a Captain, was with this army, and when the general of artillery was wounded in the fighting he took charge of the guns.

The artillery played a very important part in recapturing Toulon, and Napoleon had begun to make his reputation. In his report, the second-in-command of the army wrote: "Words fail me to describe Bonaparte's merits. He has plenty of knowledge, and as much intelligence." Augustin Robespierre, brother of Maximilien, the leading member of the Committee of Public Safety, described him as "an artillery officer of transcendent [superior] merits." Thus had the young Corsican lieutenant of artillery seized the chances offered by revolution and war and at the age of 23 was promoted to Brigadier General.

Then a sudden blow fell: the Committee of Public Safety was overthrown in July 1794 and the Robespierres and their colleagues were guillotined. Napoleon was imprisoned and for two weeks his life was in danger. Thanks to the influence of some friends he was released and he continued to make plans for Italy.

In 1795 the men who had overthrown the Jacobin government drew up a new constitution by which France was to be governed by five Directors, appointed by two elected councils. One of the Directors, Paul Barras, put Napoleon in charge of the government's armed forces in Paris. On 6th October (14th *Vendémiare* in the new revolutionary calendar) an armed mob shouting Jacobin slogans tried to overthrow the new government. Napoleon, once more in charge of the guns, quickly dispersed the rising with what he called "a whiff of grapeshot". As a reward for defending the government he was made Major General.

Before the end of this successful year Napoleon had fallen in love with Josephine Beauharnais, the beautiful widow of a general executed just before the fall of Robespierre. In the spring of 1796 she and Napoleon were married. Shortly afterwards came more promotion—he was appointed Commander of the Army of Italy.

"Can one be revolutionary enough? Marat and Robespierre, these are my saints." *Napoleon handing out revolutionary pamphlets written by himself during the siege of Toulon.*

Below The civil marriage of Napoleon and Josephine Beauharnais in 1796.

"I awake full of you ... sweet and incomparable Josephine. What a strange effect you have on my heart. Are you annoyed? Do I see you sad? Are you uneasy? My soul is broken by sorrow, and there is no repose for your friend." *Napoleon in a letter to Josephine, 1796.*

3 The Strategist

IN 1793 REVOLUTIONARY FRANCE faced a coalition (alliance) in which the main allies were Austria, Russia and England. The First Coalition, as it is now known, also included some smaller German states, Piedmont (in North Italy), Holland and Spain. At first the French position seemed hopeless: Prussian and Austrian forces with English support marched towards Paris, and the English navy controlled Toulon. Before the end of the year, the enthusiastic citizen armies of the Republic, led by their new generals and equipped by the efficient organisation of the Committee of Public Safety, made a remarkable recovery. The Prussians, Austrians and English were retreating across Belgium and Bonaparte's guns drove the English from Toulon.

The main English effort was now devoted to capturing French Colonies in the West Indies, but the Navy, in alliance with Spain and Holland, made some attempt to blockade the French coast. In spite of this a vital grain convoy got safely into Brest in June 1794. Meanwhile, the French armies everywhere made headway against the First Coalition. They overran Belgium and Holland, capturing the Dutch fleet by sending cavalry over the ice; drove the Spanish and Piedmontese from the soil of France, and invaded Germany across the Rhine. The Coalition began to collapse. Holland, Prussia and Spain all made peace with France in 1795. Only England, Austria and Piedmont were left in arms. The Directory now decided to attack Austria through her possessions in Northern Italy.

Below Napoleon at the time of the Italian campaign of 1796-97, aged twenty-six.

Above left French troops after the conquest of Holland in 1795.
Below left The capture of a Dutch fleet by French Hussars in January, 1795.

Right Napoleon as General-in-Chief of the Army of Italy.

"The Palazzo Serbelloni [*Napoleon's Headquarters in Milan*] is one of the most splendid in Milan . . . in the drawing room by which I entered Madame Bonaparte was sitting with Mme Visconti, Mme Berthier and Mme Yvan. Beyond an arch was the general . . . around him were senior officers of the town. . . . Nothing was so striking to me as the attitude of this little man, in the midst of giants dominated by his personality. . . . Never has a headquarters been more like a court. It was what the Tuileries became afterwards." *The poet Arnault describing his visit to Napoleon's headquarters in Milan, 1797.*

When he took over command of the Army of Italy two days after his marriage, Napoleon, although only 27, had a complete grasp of what he wanted to do and how he was going to do it. His mind was well trained and full of the new ideas about warfare developed in France during the past twenty years. He had had several years of combat experience and above all he possessed the practical ability to put his ideas into action.

During his year in Italy, 1796-97, he displayed the genius for strategy which made him almost invincible in the field. Mobility (*i.e.* the ability to move quickly) he believed was vital, and he proved himself able to organize lightning moves very efficiently. An enemy army could be outflanked by surprise attacks on its rear, or a force too thinly spread out could be destroyed by concentrating the weight of the French army on one weak point and then dealing with the separate sections of the enemy.

> "My Republic, in entrusting me with the command of an army, credited me with judgement enough to decide what would suit its interests without recourse to the advice of my enemy."
> *Napoleon to the King of Piedmont's representatives when drawing up the Armistice of Cherasco.*

Below A romantic view of Napoleon in Italy in 1796.

Above A cartoon by the English caricaturist Thomas Rowlandson, showing Napoleon directing the crossing of the bridge at Lodi. The popular French version of the story told that Napoleon heroically led the crossing himself.

He used the second of these methods to divide the combined armies of Austria and Piedmont in April, 1796. On 28th April Piedmont signed an armistice and withdrew from the war. Napoleon at once pursued the Austrians, who had withdrawn eastwards into Lombardy. When he crossed the River Po and threatened the Austrian line of retreat, the Austrian commander fell back to the strong fortress of Mantua. On 10th May Napoleon forced a passage across the river bridge at Lodi where he himself was in the thick of the fighting and four days later entered Milan, the capital of Lombardy.

At this point came the first signs that Napoleon was capable of taking a line independent of the Republican Directors. They wanted merely to plunder Italy and

Left One of Napoleon's generals in Germany, Jean-Victor Moreau.

use it for bargaining in peace negotiations with Austria. Napoleon wanted to destroy the entire Austrian army, thus gaining a strong position in Europe. When the Directors tried to send another general to share the Italian campaign Napoleon threatened to resign, and his masters gave way.

By forcing large sums of money out of the conquered lands Napoleon became very popular with his troops because he could pay them in silver instead of with the devalued French paper money. Although he sent large quantities of works of art home to Paris, it was obvious that the Directory was not fully in control of its general.

While Napoleon was operating in Italy two other generals, Moreau and Jourdan, were to attack the

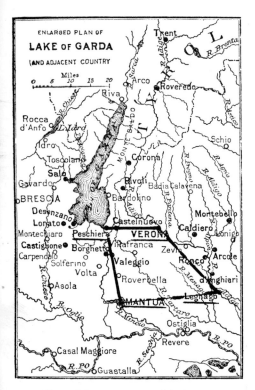

Above The area around Lake Garda, in Northern Italy, at the time of Napoleon's campaign of 1796-97. The Quadrilateral, formed by the four fortresses at Peschiera, Castelnuovo, Mantua and Legnano, is shown by the heavy lines.

Austrians on the Rhine. With the enemy being pressed on two fronts, Napoleon hoped to be able to advance from Italy, through the Tyrol towards Vienna itself. But on the Rhine the Austrians succeeded in holding up the French advance.

Napoleon himself was now forced onto the defensive. The Austrians had a very strong base in the area South of Lake Garda. This area was known as the Quadrilateral, because it was dominated by four fortresses: Peschiera, Verona, Mantua and Legnano. From this excellent position the Austrians counter-attacked four times between August 1796 and January 1797. Although he lacked reinforcements, and the Austrians had good lines of communication from the Quadrilateral to Austria itself, by making tremendous demands on his troops Napoleon converted each counter-attack into a French victory. At Castiglione he used massed artillery to disorganize the Austrian front, while at Bassano he took the Austrian commander in the rear by a surprise attack. By forcing the Bridge of Arcola across the River Adige he just succeeded in a daring attack on the Austrian flank, and once again by the concentration of his forces at Rivoli he routed the attacking Austrian forces and went on to capture Mantua. The Directory rushed reinforcements into Italy, and Napoleon pushed on into Austria, compelling her to sign an armistice at Leoben.

Napoleon was now free to complete his negotiations for the Austrian peace treaty. At Campo Formio in October 1797 Austria was forced to give her province of Belgium to France and to recognise the Cisalpine Republic. This had been created by Napoleon in 1796, out of Lombardy and several Italian states south of the Po, and some mainland territories of the Republic of Venice. By a ruthless and shameful deal, Austria accepted Venice from Napoleon as compensation, thus ending the 1,000 year history of the Republic of Venice.

What was Napoleon trying to do? Obviously his first aim was to make the position of his army in Italy quite

Left Napoleon leading the French
forces across the bridge at Arcole.

safe. But his political actions went far beyond this
objective. He had taken the political re-organization of
Italy into his own hands, regardless of the wishes of his
own government. It is clear that, although he talked of
bringing liberty to Italy, his quest for personal power
and glory was beginning to influence his every move.

4 Adventure in the Middle East

BY THE END OF 1797 France had defeated all her enemies on the Continent. Only one European country remained unconquered—England. If France was to control the whole of Europe, she would need to defeat England, and that meant an invasion.

When Napoleon returned to Paris in triumph in 1797 he was appointed Commander of the Army of England. Although he was given a first-rate army of 50,000 troops, he pointed out to the Directors that the French naval forces were quite inadequate; an attack across the Channel needed naval supremacy. His thoughts turned to a plan he had had in his mind in Italy. "The time is not far distant", he wrote to the Directors in August 1797, "when we shall feel that in order to destroy England we must occupy Egypt." The object would be to ruin English trade in the Mediterranean, and finally threaten her power and trade in India.

Napoleon wanted to act quickly. He realized how soon his glory would fade if nothing happened. The Italian successes would soon be forgotten, and the Directors would not be at all sorry to see their powerful general lose some of his popularity. He himself said, "My glory is already thread-bare. This little Europe is too small a field. Great celebrity can be won only in the East."

The Directors quickly approved his plan for a campaign in the Middle East, and Napoleon gathered his forces together. He had 38,000 troops, carried in 400 transports. He also took with him scientists and historians to explore and record the wonders of Egypt on France's behalf.

Left Napoleon's triumphant return to Paris after the signing of the Treaty of Campo Formio, October 1797.

> "Whatever efforts we make, it will be many years before we achieve supremacy at sea. To carry out an invasion of England without command of the sea is as difficult and daring a project as has ever been undertaken."
> *Napoleon in a letter to the Directory, February, 1798.*

25

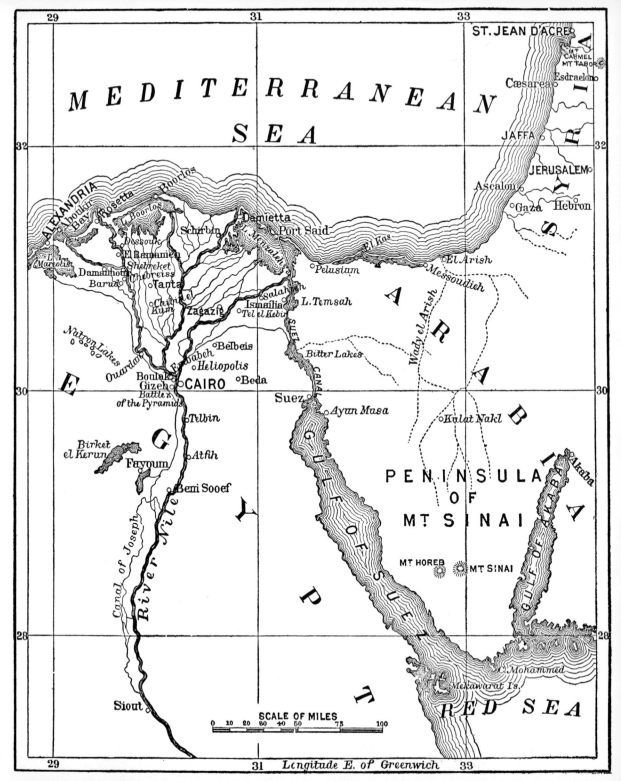

MEDITERRANEAN SEA

SYRIA

ST. JEAN D'ACRE
MT. CARMEL
MT. TABOR
Esdraelon
Cæsarea
JAFFA
JERUSALEM
Ascalon
Gaza
Hebron

ALEXANDRIA
Aboukir Bay
Rosetta
Boorlos
Boorlos
El Ramanieh
Schirbin
Damietta
Port Said
L. Menzaleh
El Kas
El Arish
Messoudieh
Pelusium
Dessouk
Shebreket Chebreiss
Tanta
Damanhour
Barud
Chibin Kum
Zagazig
Salahieh
L. Temsah
Ismailia
Tel el Kebir
Natron Lakes
Ouardan
Belbeis
Elbabeh
Heliopolis
Beda
Boulak
Gizeh
CAIRO
Battle of the Pyramids
Suez
Ayun Musa
Telbin
Bitter Lakes
Kulat Nakl
Birket el Kerun
Fayoum
Atfih
Beni Sooef

L. Mareotis

E G Y P T

Canal of Joseph
River Nile

ARABIA

Wady el Arish

PENINSULA
OF
MT. SINAI

MT. HOREB
MT. SINAI

GULF OF SUEZ

GULF OF AKABA

Akaba

C. Mohammed
Mekawarat I's.

RED SEA

Siout

SCALE OF MILES
0 10 20 30 40 50   75   100

Longitude E. of Greenwich

The expedition set sail from Toulon on 19th May, 1798, escorted by 13 warships. It reached Alexandria in July, having captured Malta from the Knights of St John *en route*. Napoleon marched his troops through the desert to Cairo and at the Battle of the Pyramids he destroyed the Mamelukes, the historic Turkish cavalry force. At once he issued a proclamation claiming to be a friend of the Sultan of Turkey (in theory Egypt was part of the Turkish Empire), and began to organize a government on French lines. But in August he heard the crushing news that by great daring and skill Lord Nelson, Admiral of the English Mediterranean fleet, had got between the French fleet and the coast of Egypt and destroyed it at the Battle of the Nile on 1st August, 1798. Although master of Egypt, Napoleon was now a prisoner there.

In the meantime the French scientists and historians established the Institute of Egypt. A printing press was set up, a geographical survey was begun, hospitals were formed and archaeologists began to explore the cities of ancient Egypt.

> "Several days ago a sickness made its appearance in the army . . . as assurances of the surgeon general failed to convince that it was not the plague, the commander-in-chief [*Napoleon*] has been to visit the hospital in person, touched the principal sufferers and helped to move the body of a soldier with swellings who had just died. This stroke of policy is having the best effects." *Brigadier Détroye.*

Below The Mamelukes, once a proud Turkish cavalry force, submitting to Napoleon in Cairo.

Above The Battle of Aboukir Bay, fought on 1st August, 1798, where Napoleon's fleet was defeated by the English Fleet under Nelson. This battle was a turning point in Napoleon's Egyptian campaign.

"Death is nothing, but to live defeated and inglorious is to die daily." *Napoleon to General Lauriston.*

Although Napoleon was re-organizing the political and social life of Egypt, he was not secure from the military point of view. He had to be prepared for Turkey to launch an attack southwards, through Asia Minor and Syria, which she owned. To avoid this he himself invaded Syria in 1799. He quickly captured Jaffa but was held up at the naval port and fortress of Acre. A British naval squadron under Sir Sidney Smith was there. It strengthened the garrison and cut Napoleon's sea communications. After two months Napoleon had to give up his siege.

Events now moved very quickly. Napoleon heard that Russia and Turkey had declared war on France and Russia had invaded Italy. In July 1799 the Turks landed an invading force in Egypt, at Aboukir Bay. With his customary skill Napoleon rushed 10,000 men to Alexandria, where they destroyed a Turkish army

nearly twice as large on 25th July, 1799.

At this point he learned that Italy had been lost to Russia and that the French General Jourdan had been defeated on the Rhine. He decided at once to return to France. In great secrecy he handed over his command to General Kléber and on 24th August set sail for France with a few generals and scientists in two frigates.

Napoleon was then, and has been since, severely criticized for "deserting" his army, but secrecy was essential if he was to slip through the English naval blockade. He knew too that Egypt could only be held if France was victorious in Europe, and Napoleon believed that his job in 1799 was to ensure that victory. More than this he had, first in Italy then in Egypt, begun to show himself as a brilliant political leader as well as a victorious army commander.

Above A cartoon by Thomas Rowlandson showing Napoleon sneaking away from his army in Egypt to return to France. This was the English view at the time, but, in fact, secrecy was essential to Napoleon's escape.

"**Instruct the officer in command of the place to decapitate all prisoners taken with arms in their hands. They are to be taken tonight to the banks of the Nile and their headless bodies thrown in the river.**" *Napoleon's instructions to Berthier about the Cairo rebels, October 1798.*

Above Napoleon dissolving the Council of the Five Hundred at
St Cloud on 10th November, 1799 (18th Brumaire).

5 The First Consul

ON 13TH OCTOBER, 1799 Paris heard that General Bonaparte had landed at St Raphael, on the south coast of France. On his journey to Paris he received a hero's welcome. News of his victory at Aboukir had recently come through, and it was generally believed that he was the man to put right what had gone wrong in Italy and elsewhere.

France's fortunes at this time were at a low point. Her enemies in Europe—England, Turkey, Austria and Russia—had joined together in the Second Coalition. In Italy she had lost Piedmont and Milan and the republics she had set up there collapsed in bloody civil war.

At home, too, there were problems. The Directors were once again under attack from the elected Councils and could not govern effectively. Bands of brigands roamed the country and trouble broke out in the west, where there had been savage fighting during the Revolution.

One of the results of the reduced power of the Directory was that it could not enforce the taxation laws effectively, and it was losing money steadily. Then, when the Italian Republics were taken, one of France's largest sources of money was lost. In 1799 the government's income was 400,000,000 francs less than its expenditure.

Not surprisingly, several groups were trying to overthrow the Directory. Napoleon would have nothing to do with those who had Jacobin ideas. Instead he joined with Emanuel Sieyès, a moderate who regarded himself as an expert constitution maker. He hoped to use Napoleon's military power to impose a

> "A constitution should be short and obscure." *Napoleon.*

> "There is your man, he will make your coup d'état better than I." *General Moreau to Sieyès when asked to join in the plot to overthrow the Directory.*

new constitution and then discard him. Napoleon had no intention of being discarded.

Between them they planned a *coup d'état,* a plot to overthrow the Directory and establish a government of three consuls. The Directors were persuaded to resign and the councils were called to meet at St Cloud, outside Paris. It was hoped that with Napoleon's younger brother Lucien as president of one of them, and surrounded by troops, the new government would be voted in "legally". There was, however, violent opposition. Napoleon, reluctant to use force, lost his nerve. But Lucien kept his head, called in the troops just in time and drove out the opposition. The remaining councillors voted in the new constitution.

Sieyès' plan was that the two new assemblies should be chosen from a "list of notabilities" drawn up by each *commune* (town) and *département* (something like our county). From this list all members of the government would be appointed. First there were three consuls. Napoleon made himself First Consul, forcing Lucien and Sieyès into the background. Sieyès was compelled

Below The two Consuls nominated with Napoleon at the *coup de Brumaire: left* Emanuel Sieyès and *right* Napoleon's younger brother, Lucien.

Above The Installation of Napoleon as First Consul,
25th December, 1799.

33

to be President of the Senate, a sort of House of Lords. This body nominated the members of the other two assemblies — the Tribunate, which discussed laws but could not vote on them, and the Legislative, which could vote on laws, but not discuss them. Since half of the Senate was nominated by the First Consul it was obvious that very soon the Consulate would become a Dictatorship.

In February 1800 the new constitution was put to a plebiscite, *i.e.* every voter could vote for or against it. 3,000,000 French citizens voted in favour, 1,500 against. In a proclamation the Consuls said, "Citizens, the Revolution is established on the principles with which it began. It is complete."

On the surface the new constitution was democratic, because it had been almost unanimously approved by the voters. But in reality the Tribunate and Legislative were powerless, and in practice the First Consul appointed all officials. Above all, the Consulate had replaced the Directory by force. On 10th November, 1799 it was the army that had tipped the scales. Although the plebiscite had proved Napoleon's popularity, his power rested firmly on the army.

Right Napoleon as First Consul of France. This portrait, by the French painter Ingres, is claimed to be one of the few for which Napoleon posed.

6 War and Peace

IN THE WINTER OF 1799 France's military position was serious. The Second Coalition (England, Turkey, Austria and Russia) was still quite strong. The French army in North Italy under General Masséna was outnumbered two to one by the Austrians under General Mélas.

At this stage Napoleon decided to order the army on the Rhine to prepare to attack across the river. He also built up a reserve army based on Dijon. This army was for Napoleon the centre of a huge front line, with its right wing on Genoa and its left on the Danube.

By the end of May 1800 the reserve army had crossed the Alps by the Great and Little St Bernard Passes. Masséna was now besieged in Genoa by Mélas, but Napoleon was able to concentrate his forces in Milan unhindered. Although Masséna had to surrender Genoa early in June, he was able to keep his army intact.

Napoleon now moved westwards from Milan, defeating an Austrian corps at Montebello. Then came Marengo, the decisive battle which was nearly a defeat for Napoleon. Wrong information led him to believe that two bridges over the River Bormida were destroyed. He tried to encircle the Austrian army under General Mélas by sending off Desaix with two divisions to the South and another to the North. Since the two bridges were intact, Mélas with his whole force of 30,000 men and 92 guns advanced on Napoleon, caught in an open plain with 22,000 men and only 15 guns. Hurriedly Napoleon recalled his three divisions, but by the time Desaix and one division reached the battle, Napoleon's troops were being driven back in disorder.

Two of Napoleon's Generals in Northern Italy: *above* André Masséna and *below* Louis-Charles-Antoine Desaix.

Below The Battle of Marengo, in which only the prompt action of General Desaix saved Napoleon from defeat.

In a desperate effort, Desaix's fresh division counter-attacked, and some extra field guns were rushed into position. Desaix was killed, but his action saved the day. The Austrians in turn were taken by surprise and defeat became victory. The next day Mélas signed an agreement by which he withdrew all his forces eastwards to Mantua.

Gradually the Second Coalition was crumbling. Austria's army on the Rhine was defeated by the French general Moreau. The Russians also withdrew, and Napoleon established French supremacy on land.

> "Few people realize the strength of mind required to conduct . . . one of those great battles on which depends the fate of an army, a nation, the possession of a throne. Consequently one rarely finds generals who are keen to give battle. . . ."
> *Napoleon at St Helena.*

But the victories of the English admiral Nelson and the surrender of the French army in Egypt ensured English supremacy at sea. Now the English Prime Minister, William Pitt, wanted to negotiate peace. The result was the Peace of Amiens, agreed in March 1802. England promised to restore Egypt to Turkey and Malta to the Knights of St John, but was allowed to keep Ceylon (taken from the Dutch) and Trinidad (taken from Spain). France, on her part, agreed to take her troops out of Rome and Naples.

Napoleon since gaining power had not only brought victory, he had brought peace! The constitution of the Consulate was changed so that he became First Consul for life (instead of ten years). France supported the change by an overwhelming majority in another plebiscite. His single-handed rule had begun.

> "The French nation longed for peace; it had received it from Bonaparte's hands. It was attached to the social achievements of the revolution; Bonaparte had preserved them."
> *G. Lefebvre, a modern French historian, on Napoleon's position after Amiens.*

7 Victory in Europe

THE PEACE OF AMIENS was destined to last only fourteen months. Who was to blame for breaking it is still a matter of debate.

Napoleon continued his occupation of Belgium and Holland. He seized Piedmont and Elba, and his naval expedition to San Domingo seemed to threaten England's trade and Empire. England retaliated by refusing to give up Malta. William Pitt spoke of "the experimental peace", and in 1803 the English ambassador left France. England began to seize French ships and Napoleon imprisoned English civilians caught in France.

Now Napoleon's thoughts turned once again to the invasion of England, and preparations began quickly. Two thousand boats were ordered and 100,000 men assembled around Boulogne to form the Army of England. Even if they did not in fact invade England, they were ready for other operations. Napoleon's dreams of almost limitless power were uppermost in his mind. In December 1804 he was crowned "Emperor of the French Republic". Until he had a son, brother Joseph was his heir.

An invasion of England needed naval control of the English Channel. Napoleon had a plan to achieve this. In December 1804 Spain joined France, and the combined French and Spanish fleets were sent to lure Nelson's fleet away from Europe by pretending to attack in the West Indies. Nelson chased the French Admiral Villeneuve there, but sent a fast ship to warn the Admiralty that the French were doubling back to the Channel. So a British squadron met Villeneuve off Cape Ushant. His ships were not in very good shape,

Below Joseph Bonaparte, brother of Napoleon and heir to the French Consulate until Napoleon had a son.

Left Lord Nelson, whose great victory in the Battle of Trafalgar ensured British naval supremacy for many years.

Above A scene from the Battle of Trafalgar, 21st October, 1805.

and after an indecisive skirmish, the French took refuge first in Corunna, and then at Cadiz.

Unwisely, Napoleon ordered Villeneuve out to fight: the result was Nelson's great victory off Cape Trafalgar on 21st October, 1805. England was safe from naval attack for many years.

Pitt, meanwhile, was building up a Third Coalition. Russia's new young Tsar Alexander I had pro-British advisers, and joined Pitt in April 1805. In May Napoleon was crowned King of Italy, and the Emperor of Austria in alarm joined the Alliance in August.

The last four months of 1805 showed Napoleon the General at his most brilliant. The allies thought Italy would be the main battleground, but Napoleon had 190,000 men over the Rhine by the end of September (including the Army of England!). Taken completely by surprise, the Austrian General Mack was trapped in Ulm on the Danube, and surrendered with 50,000 men.

Above The death of Nelson during the Battle of Trafalgar.

Below Frederick William III of Prussia. He declared war on the French in 1806, and at the Battles of Jena and Auerstädt his army was destroyed.

Kutusov and the Russians had now arrived in Austria. They joined with the Austrian forces, and managed to avoid battle with Napoleon, while he entered Vienna. Soon Napoleon was outnumbered by 90,000 Austro-Russians to just over 70,000 French fighting troops. If the King of Prussia had now joined the allies Napoleon's situation would have become very dangerous. Fortunately Frederick William, weak and selfish, remained undecided. Nevertheless the French were seriously outnumbered.

On 2nd December, 1805 the Austro-Russians advanced on the village of Austerlitz, spreading themselves out to cut off the French line of retreat. Napoleon quickly spotted that by doing this they had weakened their centre, grouped on the Pratzen Heights. He struck at once. Massed artillery followed by a powerful attack at this point cut the allied army in two.

Alexander, weeping for the thousands of Russian dead, withdrew towards Russia. Francis of Austria made the Peace of Pressburg with Napoleon, losing large areas in Venetia, Dalmatia (part of modern Yugoslavia), and the Tyrol. Three South German states which had allied with Napoleon—Bavaria, Württemberg and Baden—became independent kingdoms. And so Austria lost her influence in Germany, as she had already lost it in Italy.

In 1806 Napoleon organized sixteen German rulers into The Confederation of the Rhine which promised to support the French armies. At the end of 1805 the King of Naples was deposed and replaced by Joseph Bonaparte. Frederick William of Prussia was getting anxious, and when he was threatened with the loss of Hanover which he had taken from the English crown, he declared war on Napoleon. He was much too late. It was almost suicide for Prussia.

Without waiting for help from the Russians, the old-fashioned Prussian army lumbered into the attack. The result was inevitable: at Jena and Auerstädt the Prussian army was destroyed. Frederick William shut himself up in the fortress of Königsberg while Napoleon occupied his kingdom as a base against the Russians, who were now his main danger.

In the snows of February the French only just defeated the Russians in the hideously bloody battle of Eylau, after huge losses on both sides. But in June Napoleon caught the Russian commander Bennigsen in a dangerous position on the banks of the River Alle, near the town of Friedland. French artillery destroyed the only two bridges in the Russian rear, and 25,000 Russians were slaughtered. It was 14th June — the anniversary of Marengo. The Third Coalition was destroyed.

> **"This Battle is as decisive as Austerlitz, Marengo and Jena."**
> *Napoleon writing to Paris after Friedland.*

Left Napoleon and his staff at the Battle of Austerlitz, 2nd December, 1805.

Above French soldiers searching for English goods at Leipzig town
gate during the Continental Blockade.

8 Economic Warfare

THE SITUATION IN 1807 was similar to that of 1797—
the coalition of European powers had been destroyed
on land, but England, supreme at sea, refused to come
to terms. It was a fight between the lion and the whale.
England had always supplied large sums of money to
her continental allies. This gold came from trade.
Napoleon decided that if England's trade could be
strangled, she would go bankrupt. She would then be
unable to subsidize the European powers, and would
be compelled to submit.

Economic warfare was not a new idea. From 1793
French revolutionary governments had forbidden the
import of British goods. In 1803 Napoleon extended
this along the coast up to North West Germany. In
1806, after Jena and Auerstädt, he issued the Berlin
Decrees which proclaimed that the British Isles were in
a state of blockade: no trade with Britain was allowed,
and any goods coming from Britain or her colonies
would be seized.

In 1806 Napoleon controlled the coasts of France,
Belgium, Holland, Germany and Italy, except the
Papal States. His victory at Friedland persuaded Tsar
Alexander of Russia to make peace. On a raft in the
middle of the River Niemen the two Emperors met and
agreed to the Treaty of Tilsit. Alexander listened
eagerly to schemes by which he and Napoleon would
share the Western World. He agreed to the splitting up
of Prussia, recognized the new German Kingdom of
Westphalia with the young Jerome Bonaparte as King,
and the Grand Duchy of Warsaw (the main part of
Poland) under the King of Saxony. Above all, Russia
agreed to close her ports to English trade—to become

> "I am more alarmed than I can
> say. How will our people live?"
> *Lord Portland, British Prime
> Minister, in 1807.*

Below Jerome Bonaparte, brother
of Napoleon, whom he made King
of Westphalia.

part of Napoleon's blockade, or "Continental System".

Quickly the English government hit back with the Orders in Council at the end of 1807, which ordered all neutral ships to carry a licence in English ports. Otherwise they were lawful prize for the Royal Navy. Napoleon in turn, by the Fontainebleu and Milan Decrees, proclaimed that any neutral ship obeying the English orders would be treated as an English ship.

Did England suffer? At times her export trade declined alarmingly, especially in 1807 and 1810-11. Unemployment and bankruptcies, made worse by bad harvests, showed that Napoleon's policy could be effective. But English exports reached a record figure in 1809, and by the end of 1812 the Continental System collapsed.

To be finally successful Napoleon had to control the whole European coastline. He was led to quarrel with the Pope, to invade Spain and finally to quarrel with Alexander. Success also depended on consistency, and in order to raise money Napoleon sold licences to trade with England. In other words he was selling the right to break his own system.

Apart from the gaps in Europe, England also found eager markets for her goods in the Spanish colonies in South America, who bitterly resented Napoleon's invasion of Spain. And although trade with the United States was briefly interrupted by a war in 1812, many English goods were exported across the North Atlantic in these years.

When we add to these facts the knowledge that French overseas trade was seriously damaged by the blockade and that Europe became desperately short of colonial goods (*e.g.* sugar and cotton), we shall understand why the British economy survived.

Right The meeting of Napoleon and Alexander I of Russia on a raft on the River Niemen, 25th June, 1807. As a result of this meeting the two Emperors signed the Treaty of Tilsit. Under the terms of the treaty Russia agreed to help France against England, and particularly to enforce Napoleon's Continental Blockade.

47

9 The Politician

WE MUST NOW RETURN TO FRANCE ITSELF, and find out what Napoleon had done to improve the political situation after the fall of the Directory.

In 1800 local government and finance were re-organized. Each *commune* was to have a mayor, each *arrondissement* (rural district) a sub-prefect, and each *département* a prefect. All these agents of the central government were appointed by Napoleon, who came at the top of this pyramid of power. A brilliant financier from the days of Louis XVI, Martin Michel Charles Gaudin, became Minister of Finance. By using the new powerful system of local government, he brought taxes right up to date.

Napoleon took from Sieyès the idea of a Council of State, and collected round him a body of experts, appointed by himself, to help him decide general lines of policy. He used ex-revolutionaries, both moderate and Jacobin, alongside ex-Royalists. "I am national, I like honest men of all colours", he said. By using men of talent regardless of their past records he tried to bring about national unity. Under the energetic leadership of the First Consul, the Council burst into life, giving a new vigour to the government of France.

But if national unity was really to return to France, the deep religious split had to be healed. By 1801 Napoleon had brought peace with France's enemies—peace with the Catholic Church must be his next objective.

Since 1791 there had been two Churches in France; one was the Constitutional Church, the other was the Church of Rome. The members of the Church of Rome were those who would not swear an oath to the Constitution, but remained loyal to the Pope instead.

"The meetings [*of the Council*], made longer by Napoleon's digressions, were never too long for him.

"Anyone might ask leave to speak. Napoleon often called upon others, whose opinions he wished to know. Speeches had to be simple and straight-forward."
Pelet, a member of the Council.

In 1801 the argument between these two Churches still continued. To make matters worse, the Pope had never forgiven the French government for confiscating Church lands and taking the Church under its control in 1791. If Napoleon could bring the two Churches together, what a triumph it would be, and how his influence in all Catholic countries would increase!

After long, hard bargaining the Concordat, an agreement with Pope Pius VII, was signed. By this Roman Catholicism was recognized as the religion of the majority of French citizens. The First Consul would nominate Bishops, and his government would pay the clergy's salaries. In spite of violent opposition from ex-Jacobins (especially a number of generals) the Concordat did bring about another important element of national unity.

Below Napoleon and Pope Pius VII during their discussions at Fontainebleau. Napoleon is employing his usual tactic of violent argument, but the Pope seems rather unimpressed.

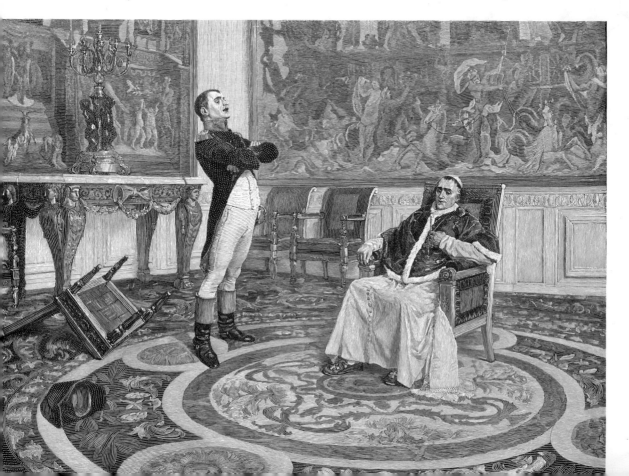

Since 1789 various revolutionary governments had been trying to draw up a single code of civil law to replace the muddle of different types of law which existed before the Revolution. Napoleon was no lawyer, but he was the driving force which led the Council of State to produce the Civil Code in 1804. This was a mixture of the traditional Roman Law, the law under which France had previously been governed, and the very free laws introduced by the Revolution. One of its main features was to strengthen the family and the powers of the father. In 1807 the civil code was re-named the *Code Napoléon*.

The Revolution had abolished all titles and honours, but in 1802 Napoleon started the Legion of Honour, believing that it was important that good service and individual glory should be rewarded. Civilians and soldiers could both gain positions in the Legion and the three senior ranks carried life pensions. The First Consul always believed that "mankind is governed with baubles".

So in a very few years the government machine had been transformed and the whole of France felt the effects of the dynamo at the centre. Napoleon the political leader tried to show that he was not a military dictator by keeping his generals out of politics. But his government was certainly a dictatorship. In 1800 when he and Josephine narrowly escaped being blown up by a bomb (planted probably by Royalist plotters), he used this as an excuse to deport 130 known Jacobins. He wanted no opposition. In January 1800 he suppressed sixty of the seventy-three newspapers in Paris.

Yet in 1802, on a wave of popularity, another huge majority in a plebiscite made Napoleon First Consul for life. His government had certainly given France "fraternity", in the sense of national unity, and "equality" in that the privileges of the monarchy had gone for ever, but "liberty" seemed to have disappeared in the First Consul's dictatorship.

Right The attack on Napoleon's life in 1800; he and the Empress Josephine escaped unharmed.

52   *Above* The coronation of Napoleon as Emperor of France in the Cathedral of Nôtre Dame, Paris, on 2nd December, 1804.   Painted by J. L. David.

10 The Emperor

FURTHER PLOTTING, by Royalists now, soon turned the Life Consul into an Emperor. In August 1803 a Royalist force landed with English help near Calais. Napoleon's cunning and efficient Chief of Police, Joseph Fouché, discovered the plot and reported that a prince of the French royal family was expected. In March 1804 the conspirators were rounded up in Paris; twelve were executed, and the others imprisoned. An exiled Jacobin, General Pichegru, had joined the Royalist plotters. He committed suicide in prison before he could be brought to trial.

But Napoleon was not satisfied: he was determined to be revenged on the House of Bourbon, the royal family of France. He believed that the mysterious prince was the young Duc d'Enghien who was living just across the frontier in the German state of Baden. The Duke was kidnapped, rushed to Paris, tried by military court under General Joachim Murat, the Governor of Paris, and executed by firing squad. Was this brutal act the code of the Corsican Vendetta working in Napoleon's mind? Europe was horrified.

Napoleon and his ministers certainly took the plots seriously—if he were assassinated chaos would break out again. To prevent this the Senate declared in May 1804 that "The Government of the Republic is entrusted to a hereditary Emperor". Until Napoleon had a son Joseph was his heir. On 2nd December, 1804, in the Cathedral of Nôtre Dame, the Pope anointed Napoleon. Amidst scenes of great splendour, Napoleon placed the imperial crown on his own head.

An Emperor needs a court. At once Napoleon began appointing court officials with high-sounding titles like

"If a man received an injury and could not find an opportunity to be revenged on his enemy personally, he revenged himself on one of his relations. So barbarous a practice was the source of innumerable assassinations." *James Boswell on Corsica; bear in mind the assassination of the Duc d'Enghien.*

"His small figure melted away under the huge ermine mantle. A plain laurel crown encircled his head. He looked like an antique medal." *Madam de Rémusat describing the Coronation.*

Above Charles Maurice-Elie, Duke of Talleyrand-Périgord, Napoleon's Foreign Minister whom he made Prince of Benevento.

Arch-Chancellor and Arch-Treasurer. Full-scale ceremonial was re-introduced to the Tuileries Palace, the home of the Kings of France where Napoleon now lived. "Kingship is an actor's part", said Napoleon. The Emperor created a whole range of nobles: Princes, Dukes, Counts, Barons, and Knights. The titles were supported by grants of lands. Marshal Bernadotte became Prince of Pontecorvo and Foreign Minister Talleyrand Duke of Benevento. By creating this new nobility Napoleon hoped to keep his generals out of politics; to persuade the old nobility to return; and to prove that the idea of nobility now had nothing to do with the old *régime* before 1789.

Another of Napoleon's Corsican characteristics was his devotion to ties of friendship and family. Even when he knew that Marshal Bernadotte was untrustworthy (he betrayed Napoleon in 1813) he still favoured the man, who was married to his first fiancée. The treatment of his family makes this characteristic very clear. Joseph, his eldest brother, was made King first of Naples, then of Spain. Another brother, Louis, was made King of Holland. The youngest Bonaparte, Jerome, was made King of Westphalia. Marshal Murat (married to Caroline Bonaparte) succeeded Joseph in Naples. Napoleon's sister, Elsa Bonaparte, became Grand Duchess of Tuscany and his stepson, Eugène Beauharnais, was made Viceroy of Italy.

All the Bonapartes were self-willed and quarrelsome, and they all caused trouble for their eminent brother. As we shall see, the idea of an Empire composed of Kings related to the Emperor did not really work. When it was all over, and Napoleon was a prisoner on the lonely island of St Helena, he remarked, "My family have not helped me".

Right Four members of Napoleon's family whom he promoted to high position after his coronation: *above left* Louis, made King of Holland; *above right* Caroline, made Queen of Naples; *below left* Elisa, made Grand Duchess of Tuscany; *below right* Eugene Beauharnais (Napoleon's stepson), made Viceroy of Italy.

11 Control of Europe

"NAPOLEON WAS ABOUT FIVE FEET SIX INCHES, and well made . . . his neck was short and his shoulders broad . . . he had a high broad forehead, a straight well-formed nose and rather fine teeth. His skin was smooth and his complexion pale . . . in short the nobility of his head and bust were unsurpassed by the finest antique busts." This is how Napoleon appeared to Claude-François Méneval, who in 1802 became his private secretary.

The man who in 1807 ruled most of Europe, although rather short in height, must have been an impressive figure. In this year his Empire was at its height, before the war in Spain and the quarrel with the Pope began to create weaknesses. Italy, Germany, Switzerland, Holland and Belgium were all under his control. Whether an area was ruled by one of his brothers or by a Marshal as King or Duke, or by a local ruler who had come to terms with Napoleon, the government of these countries was always, as in France, a disguised dictatorship.

For a time there was a good deal of co-operation from the local populations; particularly, where they existed, from the middle classes. From the early days of the wars, France had introduced the ideas of the Revolution into occupied countries. Everywhere feudalism was abolished and local assemblies were elected. The privileges of the nobles were swept away and all citizens, as in France, became equal before the law and the tax-collector.

The *Code Napoléon* and the Concordat with the Pope were introduced: vast areas of Europe were being forcibly modernized. Many merchants, professional

"In Germany, as in France, Italy and Spain, people long for equality and liberalism. The benefits of the Code Napoleon, legal procedure in open court, these are the points by which your monarchy must be distinguished." *Napoleon in a letter to Jerome, King of Westphalia.*

"The first thing you ought to have done was to introduce conscription. What can you possibly do without an army?" *Napoleon in a letter to Louis, King of Holland.*

Left Napoleon as Emperor of France. Painted by Robert Lefèvre.

men, artists, and thinkers like the great German writer Goethe were impressed, and looked forward, under Napoleon's leadership, to a more progressive way of life, which would be based on the principles of the Revolution—liberty, equality, fraternity.

Beethoven the great composer turned against Napoleon in 1804. He was disgusted at the murder of the Duc d'Enghien, and believed that by becoming Emperor Napoleon had turned into a tyrant. What was Napoleon's aim? Was he really trying to bring to Europe the benefits of the new France, or was he merely trying to extend his own power and glory, driven on by an ambition that could never be satisfied? Or again, was this control of Europe simply a necessary result of the French revolutionary wars? To defeat England, Europe must be closed to her, and so one country after another had to be taken over.

Certainly very few Europeans supported Napoleon at the end—they had been too badly hit by the economic effects of the Continental System. As we saw in Chapter 8, serious hardships were caused by the shortage of colonial goods like sugar, and by high prices.

Throughout the years of economic warfare Napoleon insisted that France must be the most favoured country in the Empire. So European trade was arranged for the benefit of France, sometimes at considerable cost to the Germans, Italians or Dutch. It is curious that Napoleon was so blind to the needs of his "satellite" states: while he was apparently creating a European empire, he was at the same time sowing the seeds of discontent among the members of that Empire and making them jealous of France.

It is true that the peoples of Europe learned a lot from the new French systems of law and taxation, but as Napoleon's wars continued they had less acceptable French ideas thrust upon them, as well as the Continental System. The system of taxation might be modern and fair, but the amount of taxes raised became increasingly heavy, and to maintain the strength of his armies Napoleon imposed conscription—

forcing people to join the army. Young men from Italy and Germany were called up to fight in Spain, in Russia—wherever the Emperor commanded.

In spite of the considerable benefits received during the period 1795-1808, the effects of the continuing warfare prevented Napoleon from gaining any real loyalty from the peoples of Europe. Indeed towards the end of the Empire, French troops and officials were generally hated.

Above A page of Beethoven's manuscript for his Third Symphony, *Eroica.* Beethoven originally dedicated the symphony to Napoleon, but crossed out the dedication in a fury when he heard of the execution of the Duc D'Enghein. To him Napoleon was now just a tyrant.

12 The Empire Style

THE FRENCH REVOLUTION had destroyed the styles and fashions of the eighteenth-century French monarchy. The Napoleonic Empire produced a new style which was in many ways influenced by the Emperor himself, and by his victories.

In the Empire of Ancient Rome military successes were celebrated by buildings. So it was with the Napoleonic Empire. The Arc de Triomphe, the Arch of Austerlitz, the Temple of the Grande Armée and the Rue de Rivoli all celebrated Napoleon's victories. The style of these buildings owed a lot to their Roman and Greek fore-runners. It is clear that Napoleon and his architects had the classical world well in mind.

A similar spirit is visible in the spectacular paintings full of movement and colour created by artists like J. L. David and Le Gros. David's vast picture of Napoleon's

Opposite page The Arc de Triomphe in Paris, built to commemorate Napoleon's great victories.

Left Jacques Louis David, French painter, whose great paintings of Revolutionary France led him to be dubbed "the Artist of the Revolution".

Above The Paris Opera in 1789. Napoleon had a great love of opera, especially Italian.

coronation, and Le Gros' vivid representation of the battles of Aboukir and Eylau are both grand and heroic. The elegance and delicacy of eighteenth-century furniture was replaced by stiffer, grander, straight-backed chairs and settees, suitable for military heroes. But although severe in shape, they were lavishly decorated with gold and ormolu (gilt metal), as befitted the designs of the Grand Empire.

"The opera is the soul of Paris as Paris is the soul of France", said Napoleon, who loved music, especially Italian opera. He visited the opera frequently to enjoy the works of composers such as Méhul and Spontini, which frequently told stories of Roman Generals, Celtic chieftains, and Spanish conquerors in South

Left Voltaire, whose dramatic works for the stage pleased Napoleon's sense of the epic and heroic.

> "Question. What should one think of those who would fail in their duties to our Emperor?
>
> "Answer. According to the Apostle St Paul, they would resist the order established by God himself, and would be deserving of eternal damnation."
>
> *From the new catechism of 1806, for primary schools.*

America. The Grande Armée went into battle accompanied by the most stirring military music in Europe!

Napoleon's favourite poems were those of the ancient Celtic poet Ossian. On the stage he liked tragic dramas such as Voltaire's *Death of Caesar* or Corneille's *Horace*. The playwrights of the Empire concentrated on grand, heroic stories.

The Emperor admitted that he hated insults: this was one of the main reasons why press censorship was introduced, as well as to maintain military security. During the Consulate the number of Parisian newspapers was reduced from seventy-three to thirteen, and by 1811 there were only four. Napoleon

Below Wash-basin designed by Percier and Fontaine for Napoleon and the Empress Josephine about 1800, with medallions of the imperial couple decorating the base.

himself took a personal interest in the government's official journal, *Le Moniteur*. To the Director-General of Censorship of books the Emperor wrote that "Everything should be printed except obscene works and those which tend to disturb the public peace."

The Empire style, then, believed in rules, and thought that society in general was more important than the individual. It believed in grandeur, honour, patriotism, courage and the family. Opposition to these beliefs came from the "Romantics", who believed that the individual was more important than society and its rules. Napoleon quarrelled violently with the leading Romantics such as Chateaubriand, who was not allowed to take his seat in the French Academy—the highest honour a writer could receive. He also exiled the rich and talented romantic writer, Madame de Staël, who, from her estate in Switzerland, helped to lead the intellectual, "liberal" opposition to Napoleon.

Internal achievements under the Empire were far less constructive than the reforms of the Consulate. The leader of France was more and more concerned with war and glory. In 1804 the Ministry of Police was revived and in 1810 political prisons were established. Now enemies of the system could be imprisoned without trial. The Empire was becoming increasingly tyrannical, using methods similar to those of the *Ancien Régime,* and of course to twentieth-century dictatorships.

In 1808 Napoleon created the University of France, a sort of Ministry of Education to control all levels of education. He hoped that the new secondary schools, the *lycées,* specially designed to produce officers and civil servants, would replace the private secondary schools run by the Church. This did not happen, but his plan for a unified system of state education has been important in France right down to the present day.

It is clear that as Emperor, Napoleon became increasingly dictatorial and self-willed. Towards the end of the Empire able men like Talleyrand and

Fouché had been replaced by lesser men who simply said "yes". The future novelist Stendhal said about these later ministers, "Napoleon had no men of ability because he wanted none." Instead of the vigorous young consul leading a group of able, energetic and talented advisers, we begin to see the fat, ageing Emperor who would listen to no-one but himself, who thought he could achieve anything and everything. This deterioration in his character led almost inevitably to the making of the great mistakes which finally brought disaster.

> "Already the young First Consul was gone, whom I had seen for the first time striding nimbly through the Tuileries, slim and easy with olive complexion. Even outwardly all was changed. His bust was short and thick, his little legs fleshy, his complexion livid, his brow bald." *The Duc de Broglie describing the Emperor on his way to Bayonne, 1808.*

Left Corneille (1606-84), another of Napoleon's favourite dramatists, reading his tragedy *Polyeucte* to a group of admirers.

66   *Above* The Madrid rising of May 1808, vividly portrayed by the Spanish artist Goya.

13 The Spanish Ulcer

CHARLES IV, his selfish Queen Maria Luisa and her lover Manuel de Godoy misruled Spain. Napoleon believed that an efficient government could make Spain prosperous and strong. Also Spain and Portugal must be controlled if the Continental System was to be complete. For these reasons, in 1807, Napoleon ordered Spain to join the System, and sent an army under Jean Junot through Spain to invade Portugal and stop her trading with England.

Obligingly Charles IV of Spain quarrelled with his son Ferdinand; Napoleon sent them to Bayonne and forced both of them to abdicate. Joseph Bonaparte was summoned from Naples to become King of Spain, and a modern French-type constitution was drawn up. But in May 1808 Madrid rose in violent protest against the exile of the royal family and Murat, the "Emperor's Lieutenant" had to use his troops to restore French control. Unwisely Napoleon did not take this rising seriously.

Throughout Spain local committees of nobles and clergy, called "Juntas", organized rebellion. Junot was defeated in Portugal by an English expeditionary force, while in Southern Spain French troops under Dupont had to surrender to the Spaniards at Baylen — the first defeat for Napoleon's soldiers. The news echoed round Europe.

In Autumn 1808 Napoleon himself took charge and entered Madrid. General Moore, the English commander in Portugal, had advanced into Northern Spain, but was forced to retreat to Corunna on the North West tip of the country, where he was killed; his troops were evacuated by sea. With the Emperor in

> "God has given me the will and force to overcome all obstacles." *Napoleon in his proclamation to the people of Madrid, 1808.*
>
> "... take care you don't destroy the spirit of the army by refusing to allow retaliation upon the Spaniards. It is impossible to show consideration towards brigands who murder my wounded, and commit every kind of outrage." *Napoleon to Joseph, King of Spain.*

Below The English General Sir John Moore, killed in 1808 at Corunna.

Above Napoleon in 1809, aged forty.

Spain all appeared secure, but with Austria appearing to be making threats he returned to Paris early in 1809, leaving Marshal Soult in command.

Without Napoleon the situation soon grew worse. General Wellesley (later Duke of Wellington) drove Soult out of Portugal, and during the next three years held on and built up his forces there. Wellington's presence kept up the spirits of the Spaniards, who were also stirred by Napoleon's treatment of the Pope. Rome had not co-operated in the Continental System, so Pope Pius VII was arrested in 1809. His states, which stretched across Central Italy, were seized. To the deeply religious Spanish peasants and their priests this was an unforgivable sin. The guerrilla bands, hiding out in the mountains, flung themselves savagely on French outposts, depots and lines of communication with a violence which frightened even the most hardened French troops.

French operations were also seriously handicapped by Napoleon's insistence on running the war from France. Orders were always out-of-date, even if the messengers managed to escape the Spanish guerrillas. The French marshals quarrelled jealously with each other and tried to avoid doing anything which might bring success to a rival.

Masséna's large army dwindled away in the bare countryside (devastated by the English troops), outside Wellington's defensive lines of Torres Vedras in 1810-11. In the following year the English general captured important fortresses on the Portuguese-Spanish border and then inflicted a large-scale defeat on Marshal Marmont at Salamanca. Neither Masséna nor Marmont would help the other general.

Finally, during that fatal year of 1812, Napoleon had to withdraw troops from Spain for his Russian campaign. So he set off to the East of Europe with his ulcer in the West still unhealed—a very dangerous situation.

14 The Awakening of Europe

IN 1808, a year after their meeting at Tilsit, Napoleon and Alexander met once again at the Conference of Erfurt; but their friendship had cooled considerably. Alexander's mother and many Russian nobles were violently anti-French. Napoleon's foreign minister, the clever but unscrupulous Talleyrand, was beginning to play false: he believed that the unending wars and extension of French power must stop and he secretly encouraged Alexander to stand up to Napoleon. As a result the conference was an empty show, and Alexander promised the French nothing more than neutrality in any future war.

"You are a violent man, I am an obstinate one. Passion is therefore wasted on me. Let us talk reason, or I am going."
Alexander to Napoleon at Erfurt, reported by General Coulaincourt, French ambassador to Russia.

Below Napoleon receiving the Austrian Minister de Vincent during the Conference of Erfurt.

Above Archduke Charles of Austria, who resisted Napoleon in 1808-09, but was defeated in the Battle of Wagram.

Encouraged by the news of the French army's surrender at Baylen, anti-French feeling began to stir in Germany. In Prussia Baron Stein and Prince Charles Hardenberg were trying to rebuild Prussia. Stein brought about laws to free the serfs and reform local government. Hardenberg re-organized the army. Some German romantics were even beginning to talk of German national unity. But in 1808 Napoleon forced King Frederick William to dismiss Stein, and German patriots began to look to Austria. Here the Archduke Charles had modernized the army and the Chancellor (the chief minister) Stadion allowed a propaganda campaign against the French, calling for loyalty to the Emperor. The example of Spanish patriotism was emphasized, and Beethoven provided the Austrian army with patriotic songs.

Faced with these threats Napoleon withdrew troops from Spain and built up an army of 300,000 for Central Europe. When war broke out between France and Austria in April 1809, although Napoleon outmanoeuvred Archduke Charles, the Austrians withdrew successfully. Napoleon once again entered Vienna. He advanced across the Danube, and was caught in a very dangerous position when he seized the Island of Lobau in the middle of the river. Charles destroyed the bridge by sending down heavy loaded barges. With tremendous skill Napoleon turned Lobau into a fortress. He repaired the bridge, summoned up reinforcements and launched a major attack on the Austrians based on the village of Wagram. Once again Napoleon found the enemy's weak spot in the centre of their line and won a victory, but at great cost. Both sides lost 20,000 men and Austrian morale had been very high.

Without help from any other power, the Austrians submitted and signed the peace of Schönbrunn. Under this agreement they lost more land, had to pay 85 million francs to France and promised to rejoin the Continental System.

The Austrian Prince Clement Metternich, who

Above Napoleon at the Battle of Wagram.

replaced Stadion, and the Emperor Francis, now decided to try to replace Russia as Napoleon's ally. They seized their opportunity in 1809, when Napoleon divorced Josephine because she had failed to give him an heir. He wanted to marry a Russian princess, but when he was turned down, he looked to Austria. Francis agreed at once that his daughter the Archduchess Marie Louise should become the new Empress of France.

Right The marriage of Napoleon and Marie Louise, daughter of the Austrian Emperor Francis, in March 1810.

The Austrian marriage in 1810 made it quite clear that the alliance with Russia was nearly finished. The Russian nobles were now even more anti-French and the merchants hated the Continental System, which stopped their trade with England. The two emperors also quarrelled over who should take Constantinople when they divided the world between them.

In 1810 Alexander broke the Continental System and Napoleon soon decided that he could not avoid a final showdown with Russia. One final war would settle everything, seal the gaps in the Continental System, and bring England to her knees. So, in spite of the unfinished war in Spain, in June 1812 Napoleon declared war on Russia.

15 Disaster in Russia

ON 25TH JUNE, 1812 Napoleon crossed the River Niemen with his Grand Army of 450,000. He probably had too many men, because in spite of tremendous organization, supplies broke down. Thousands went pillaging and deserted, so that Napoleon already suffered heavy losses without fighting any battles.

The Russians were so heavily outnumbered that they had to retreat. At Vilna and again at Vitebsk, on the Moscow road, Napoleon was unable to bring them to a pitched battle; and in the vast spaces of Russia Napoleon's skill at rapid movement was of little value. Owing to the enormous wastage and shortage of supplies at Vitebsk, Berthier and Murat begged him to halt the campaign, but he insisted on going ahead. At Smolensk he failed yet again to encircle the Russians, and captured merely a burnt-out shell of a town.

> "Bah! a battle will dispose of the fine resolution of your friend Alexander and his fortifications of sand. He is false and feeble." *Napoleon to Coulaincourt, who warned Napoleon of the dangers of invading Russia, June 1811.*

Left The burning of Smolensk in 1812. Napoleon pursued the Russian army across Russia, unable to bring them to pitched battle, and captured only deserted and burning towns and villages.

> "The system which has made Wellington victorious in Spain and exhausted the French army is what I intend to follow—avoid pitched battles and organize long lines of communication for retreat." *Alexander in a letter to the King of Prussia.*

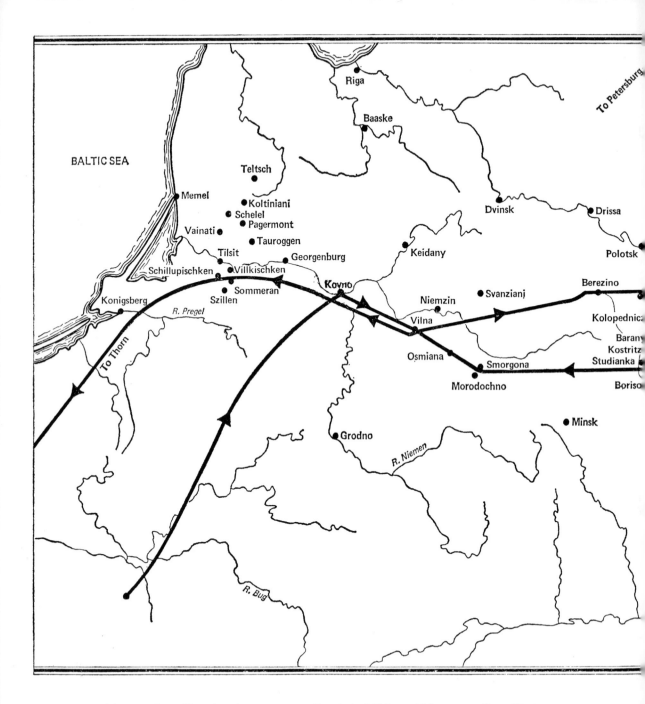

This map shows Napoleon's route across Russia in 1812, and his retreat from Moscow.

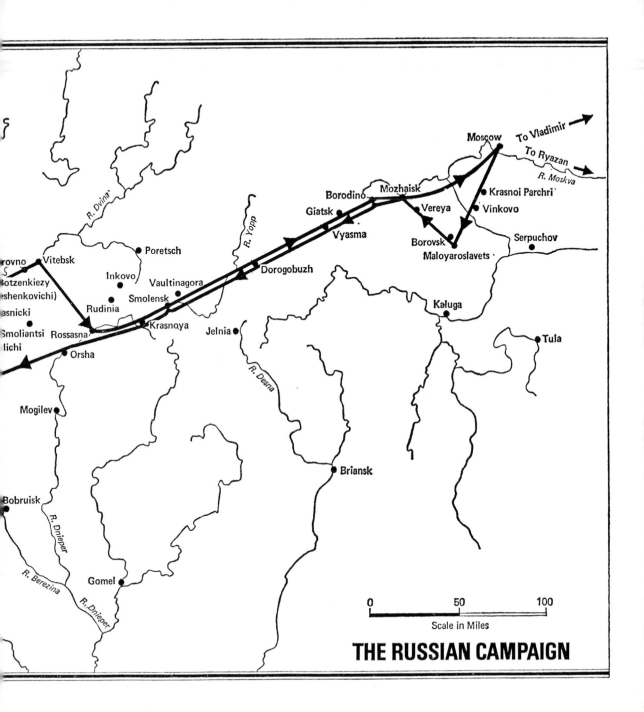

THE RUSSIAN CAMPAIGN

To Vladimir

To Ryazan

Moscow

Krasnoi Parchri

Vinkovo

Mozhaisk

Vereya

Borodino

Serpuchov

Giatsk

Borovsk

Maloyaroslavets

Vyasma

Dorogobuzh

Kaluga

R. Yopp

Poretsch

Vitebsk

Inkovo

Vaultinagora

rovno

Tula

Botzenkiezy

(shenkovichi)

Rudinia

Smolensk

Jelnia

asnicki

Krasnoya

Smoliantsi

Rossasna

lichi

Orsha

Mogilev

Briansk

Bobruisk

R. Dvina

R. Desna

R. Moskva

R. Dnieper

R. Berezina

Gomel

R. Dnieper

0   50   100

Scale in Miles

With his fighting troops reduced to 160,000 Napoleon continued to advance through a devastated land until he met the Russian army under General Kutusov defending the line of the River Moskova at Borodino. Here Napoleon fought perhaps his most desperate battle. He was ill, he refused to use his crack troops, the Imperial Guard, and although the French remained in possession of the field they lost 30,000 men.

On 14th September Napoleon saw the spires of Moscow and, according to Marshal Ney, "His joy was overflowing". But he continued in his letter to his wife, "Alas! how short was the moment of happiness!" Moscow was a deserted town. The French troops ran riot, looting and drinking; the Russians set fire to the town which burned for five days; and for five weeks Napoleon waited for Russian representatives to come and negotiate. They never came!

Napoleon seemed not to understand the danger of staying in Moscow until winter began: October 1812 was very mild. Not until 19th October did he begin to leave Moscow by a southern route, to avoid the barren

Below Marshal Ney heroically defending the rear-guard of the French Grand Army during the retreat from Moscow.

way by which he had come. But his army of 100,000, carrying masses of loot and many sick and wounded, was forced back on to the route by fierce Russian attacks at Malojaroslavetz.

Before the first snow fell the French army was collapsing from hunger and the attacks of the fierce Russian cavalry, the Cossacks. French horses died of starvation, and the French soldiers on foot found that there was nothing to eat even when they reached Smolensk. Only the Emperor's calm and skill, and the heroism of Marshal Ney commanding the rearguard, got the army as far as the Beresina. The crossing of the river brought huge losses, and when real winter arrived in early December, with 30° of frost, the suffering of the French became intolerable and their position hopeless.

Finally, on 6th December, Napoleon left his army in the hands of Murat and returned to Paris to prove to France that he was still alive and to start raising another army. When Ney led the rearguard over the Niemen and the stragglers regrouped, less than 40,000 men of the Grand Army still survived.

"I thought I should have been able to make peace, and that the Russians were anxious for it. I was deceived and deceived myself." *Napoleon in the sleigh returning to Paris, reported by Coulaincourt, who travelled with him.*

Below The horrors of the French retreat from Moscow during the bitter Russian winter. The men in the foreground are eating the raw meat of a dead horse to stay alive. Other men lie stripped of their uniforms, taken to keep someone else warm.

16 The End of the Emperor

BY FEBRUARY 1813 Napoleon in Paris was busy re-building his army to face the Russians, who were crossing into Germany. Alexander was beginning to see himself as the saviour of Europe, and signed an alliance with Frederick William of Prussia.

Everything now depended on Austria. Would Napoleon's father-in-law, the Austrian Emperor Francis, remain neutral? Desperate negotiations took place between Napoleon and Metternich, the Austrian foreign minister. Napoleon refused to give up any part of his Empire in Germany or Poland, in spite of the growing suspicion in France that he was preparing to fight for his own prestige rather than for the benefit of France. Negotiations broke down and by April 1814 Napoleon had 150,000 men in Germany—but he was desperately short of cavalry, having lost 80,000 horses in Russia.

Right Napoleon in 1813, after the heavy defeat in Russia.

"For the last two years, we've been harvesting men three times a year." *The Legislative assembly's protest against conscription in 1813.*

With less than his usual brilliance Napoleon fought two battles against the Russians and Prussians in April and May, at Lützen and Bautzen, both of which were technical victories, although incomplete. On both occasions his encircling movements were unsuccessful.

Nevertheless the Allies were shaken and Russia and Prussia signed an armistice. Once again Metternich was the chief negotiator, and he refused to give way, saying to Napoleon, "Between Europe and the aims you have hitherto pursued is an absolute contradiction. Your treaties have never been more than a truce". At this point came news of the final collapse of French power in Spain, with Wellington's victory at Vittoria. A Peace Congress organised by Metternich at Prague was a sham, with both sides merely building up their forces.

When fighting broke out again Napoleon had to face Russia, Prussia, Austria and the Swedes led by their new king, Napoleon's ex-Marshal Bernadotte. From his base at Dresden, Napoleon struck out in different directions, losing many men and exhausting his Marshals. Finally in October he fell back upon Leipzig, where the allied armies succeeded in joining up. For three days "the battle of the nations" raged, but finally the French had to retreat, losing 60,000 men.

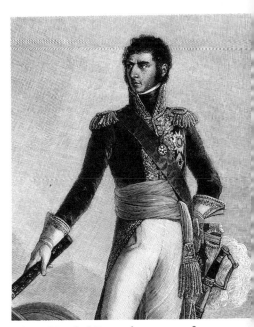

Above Marshal Bernadotte, one of Napoleon's generals, later to become King Charles XIV of Sweden.

Below The retreat of the French army from Leipzig, 19th October, 1813.

Above A poster put up in London announcing the defeat of Napoleon and the capture of Paris by the Allies on 30th March, 1814

"**Let them know that I am still the same man as I was at Austerlitz and Wagram. I want no tribunes of the people: let them know I am the great tribune.**" *Napoleon writing on 11th March, 1814.*

Now the Allies offered peace on the basis of the "natural frontiers of France" — that French rule should be limited to the boundaries formed by the Rhine, the Alps, and the Pyrenees. While Napoleon hesitated, the Senate and the Legislative Assembly in Paris called on him to accept, and began to ask for civil and political liberties. Soon the Allies, encouraged by England, hardened their offer, and when Napoleon remained obstinate, their armies invaded France's eastern territories.

War weariness was making itself felt. Wellington, now in Southern France, reported: "all except the officials are sick of Bonaparte because there is no prospect of peace with him." There was no popular rising against the foreign enemy: the spirit of 1792 had been crushed by Napoleon's dictatorship. The great French novelist Stendhal wrote, "In January 1814 the most vital people in Europe were, as a nation, nothing better than a corpse."

Yet suddenly Napoleon recovered his youthful brilliance, and although outnumbered by four to one, in lightning moves inflicted two alarming defeats on the Allies as they advanced on Paris. If the capital had held out the Allies' position would have been dangerous. But the Empress and her son left the city, Talleyrand was secretly negotiating with the enemy, and King Joseph was arguing in favour of peace. The Emperor's victories, therefore, were all in vain, for Paris surrendered on 30th March and on 1st April Talleyrand persuaded the Senate to vote the Emperor's deposition and recall Louis XVIII.

Desperately Napoleon clung to the hope of the army's loyalty, but the Marshals rebelled and refused to march. At this Napoleon signed an abdication conditional on the recognition of his son as his successor. Then news arrived that Marshal Marmont and his troops were going over to the Austrians. Napoleon could do no more — he signed an outright abdication.

17 Elba—and Waterloo

IN APRIL 1814 Napoleon and the Allies signed a treaty by which he became Emperor of Elba, a tiny island off the Italian coast near Piombino. Separated from his wife and son, he travelled through France, meeting great hostility from the population as he moved south. He worked with restless energy in his tiny kingdom, improving agriculture, organising refuse collection, and building up a miniature army and a navy of four ships!

> **"Go my son, fulfil your destiny. You were not made to die on this Island."** *Napoleon's mother on Elba.*

Left A cartoon showing Napoleon as Governor of the Island of Elba. His hat is formed by the French eagle, wounded and crouching; his throat is the Red Sea, representing his drowning armies; his face is formed by "carcases of the unhappy victims to his cruel ambition"; his hand is "judiciously placed as the epaulet drawing the Rhenish Confederacy under the flimsy symbol of the cobweb"; the spider is "a symbolic emblem of the vigilance of the Allies".

From the gardens of his house in Porto Ferraio the coast of Italy is clearly visible. Campbell, the English commissioner on Elba, warned the English government that Napoleon might well attempt an escape to Italy. The news from France gave him every encouragement to do so. The restored government of the fat, gouty Bourbon King Louis XVIII was becoming increasingly unpopular. The returned *émigré* noblemen treated Napoleon's officers with contempt: many soldiers were demobilized and 30,000 officers of the Imperial Guard were put on half pay. Many Frenchmen began to wish for Napoleon's return. Still further encouraged by the news that the Allies were quarrelling among themselves at their peace conference at Vienna, Napoleon made his plans.

Taking advantage of Campbell's absence on a short visit to Italy, Napoleon organized a small fleet of seven ships which slipped out of Porto Ferraio harbour on the 26th February. On the 1st March he landed at Cap d'Antibes, to challenge the whole of France with a thousand men!

He advanced along the mountain road through Grasse to Grenoble — now called the "Route Napoléon." Outside Grenoble an infantry regiment barred his way. Advancing alone towards them he

Right Napoleon received with ecstasy by French soldiers on his return to French soil from Elba.

82

shouted, "Kill your Emperor if you wish." At once the soldiers broke into shouts of, "Vive l'Empéreur", and the whole garrison of Grenoble went over to him. When Marshal Ney rallied to Napoleon, Louis XVIII fled towards the Allies in Belgium, 24 hours before Napoleon entered the Tuileries in triumph.

But there was no question of a restoration of the despotism of the Empire. To retain support Napoleon had to promise to rule as a constitutional monarch with an elected parliament, and with guarantees of civil liberty.

Below Napoleon's triumphant arrival at the Tuileries on his return from Elba.

Above The Prussian field-marshal Blücher, whose army was of great help to Wellington in his defeat of Napoleon at Waterloo.

> "It was the most desperate business I ever was in: I never took so much trouble about any battle, and never was so near being beat. . . . I never saw the infantry behave so well."
>
> *Wellington, the day after Waterloo, 1815.*

The sudden return of the common enemy restored unity among the Allies at Vienna. Napoleon was proclaimed an outlaw, and "delivered to public vengeance". The allied forces were mobilized. Wellington commanded a mixed force of about 100,000, while Blücher had a Prussian army of 120,000. Both forces were stationed along the Belgian Frontier.

With his old flair for speed and surprise Napoleon struck first and on the 15th June he had 120,000 men across the frontier before Wellington or Blücher knew he was attacking. His plan as usual was to get between his enemies and defeat them separately.

At first things went well: Ney attacked Blücher's Prussians at Ligny and forced them to retire. The next day Napoleon detached 30,000 men under Marshal Emmanuel Grouchy to pursue the Prussians, who in fact, were by no means routed. Heavy thunderstorms delayed French action against Wellington, who concentrated 67,000 men on rising ground near the village of Waterloo. On the morning of 18th June Napoleon faced him with 74,000.

The Emperor made two mistakes. He thought, wrongly, that the Prussians would not recover in time to help Wellington; secondly, he underestimated the fire-power of the British infantry. In the afternoon of 18th June first the French infantry and then the cavalry were worn down and repulsed, with very heavy losses on both sides. When the Prussians began to arrive precious French reserves had to be used up, and Napoleon was reluctant to send in the Guard for the final assault. When at last he did, these hitherto invincible soldiers were beaten back. The news, "the Guard is retreating" broke French morale, and when Wellington's cavalry charged, Napoleon's army fled in panic.

On 22nd June, back in Paris, Napoleon signed his second abdication, proclaiming his son Emperor Napoleon II. His political life was over.

Right Two scenes from the Battle of Waterloo: *above* the meeting of Wellington and Blücher; *below* Wellington leads the cavalry charge which routed the French forces.

18 The Last Days and the Legend

INSTEAD OF TRYING TO ESCAPE from France after Waterloo, Napoleon threw himself on the mercy of the British government. He wrote a personal letter to the Prince Regent asking to live privately in England. Having embarked on *HMS Bellerephon* he was taken to Plymouth, where the ship was surrounded with sight-seers. But he was an allied prisoner and it was England's job to find him a prison. The prison chosen was the small lonely island of St Helena in the South Atlantic used by Britain as a port of call for ships going to and from India. He was allowed three officers and twelve servants.

Right Napoleon aboard the *Bellerephon* at Plymouth, where he proved to be the biggest tourist attraction of the season.

For a few months he appeared to be not unhappy, making friends with the few English people who lived there, especially the family of William Balcombe, the East India Company agent. He seemed almost in holiday mood when he played with the sixteen-year-old Betsy Balcombe and helped her with her French.

But in April 1816 the mean-minded Hudson-Lowe, whom Wellington had dismissed from his staff as "a damned fool", arrived as governor. He was fussy and unimaginative in carrying out his orders. Napoleon was confined to the grounds of Longwood (his house); all his correspondence was to go through the governor and his presence was to be checked twice a day by the orderly officer. Napoleon, outraged, lost his temper and from August 1816 never met Lowe again.

The isolation of Longwood from the rest of the island had a bad effect on the nerves and tempers of Napoleon's staff, and several had to be dismissed. Owing to the restrictions he gave up riding and the resulting lack of exercise caused a decline in his physical condition.

Above Sir Hudson Lowe, governor of St Helena during Napoleon's last days.

Below Napoleon on his deathbed.

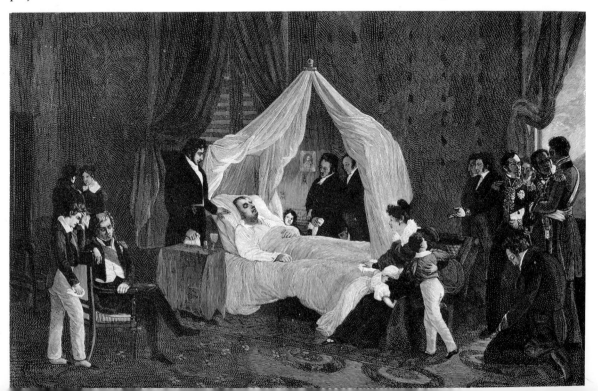

In 1817 his Doctor, O'Meara, began to treat Napoleon for jaundice. When he was dismissed by Lowe in 1818 O'Meara reported that this disease of the liver was well-advanced and that to remain in the unhealthy climate of St Helena would endanger Napoleon's life. For a year, however, he appeared to have recovered and became very busy re-organizing the Longwood garden. But from October 1820 he became ill again, and he died on 5th May, 1821 — probably from cancer of the stomach.

The Napoleonic legend began when the Emperor took an emotional farewell of his Old Guard before he left for Elba. It gathered strength as the peoples of Europe fretted against the return to the Old Regime established by the monarchs restored by the Treaty of Vienna. Young men who had not seen the horror of the Napoleonic battlefields, and who despised the backwardness of the restored rulers began to think enviously of the great days of the Empire.

Later Napoleon's memoirs encouraged the idea that he had wanted to develop national feeling among the peoples of Europe, but the nationalism of nineteenth-century Europe was quite opposed to any ideas of a European Empire. Once again we can see that Napoleon's ideas and actions were full of contradictions. Remember the contrast between his Imperial aims and the favouritism shown to France which we discussed in Chapter 11. Nevertheless, the legend was strong enough in France to sweep his nephew Louis-Napoleon to power after the revolution of 1848 and to make him Emperor Napoleon III in 1852.

Military genius, great administrator, political genius: what *was* Napoleon? His most permanent achievement was almost certainly his legal, local government, and administrative reforms in France, which gave France many long-lasting institutions. If he had not made such drastic errors in the last few years of his rule, Napoleon II might well have succeeded Napoleon I and ruled over a stable, well-organized state.

No-one ever has or ever will be able to sum up Napoleon—he was so many-sided. Perhaps it is best to let Talleyrand's words end this book. "He was clearly the most extraordinary man that has ever lived in our age, or for many ages."

Above Napoleon's corpse resting at Longwood House on the island of St Helena.

Principal Characters

ALEXANDER I (1775-1825). Emperor of Russia. Negotiated Treaty of Tilsit in 1807, waged war against Napoleon in 1812.

BARRAS, PAUL (1755-1829). A member of the Directory. Friend of Josephine Bonaparte and patron of Napoleon as a young officer.

BEAUHARNAIS, EUGÈNE DE (1781-1824). Napoleon's step-son and Viceroy of Italy.

BEAUHARNAIS, JOSEPHINE (1763-1814). Widow of Vicomte of Beauharnais and Napoleon's first wife. Married in 1796, divorced in 1810.

BERTHIER, LOUIS ALEXANDRE (1763-1815). Prince of Wagram and Neuchâtel, Napoleon's Chief of Staff.

BERNADOTTE, CHARLES (1763-1844). Marshal of France. Became heir to the throne of Sweden, and joined the allies against Napoleon in 1813.

BLÜCHER, GEBHARD-LEBERECHT VON (1742-1819). The Prussian General who gave vital support to Wellington at Waterloo.

BONAPARTE, JEROME (1784-1860). Napoleon's youngest brother, whom he made King of Westphalia in 1807.

BONAPARTE, JOSEPH (1768-1844). Napoleon's eldest brother, whom he made King of Naples in 1806 and King of Spain in 1808.

BONAPARTE, LOUIS (1778-1846). Brother of Napoleon. He married Hortense de Beauharnais (Napoleon's step-daughter).

BONAPARTE, LUCIEN   (1775-1840).   Brother   of Napoleon. Played an important part in the *coup de Brumaire.*

CHARLES, ARCHDUKE OF AUSTRIA (1771-1848). Commander of the Austrian armies in Italy and Germany.

FRANCIS II (1768-1835). Emperor of Austria, father of Marie Louise, Napoleon's second wife.

FREDERICK WILLIAM III (1770-1840). King of Prussia. Heavily defeated by Napoleon in 1806.

MARIE LOUISE HABSBURG (1791-1847). Archduchess of Austria, daughter of Francis II. Napoleon's second wife, married in 1810.

METTERNICH-WINNEBURG, CLEMENT, PRINCE OF (1773-1859). Chancellor of Austria; chief Austrian diplomat in the Napoleonic period.

MURAT, JOACHIM (1767-1815). Marshal of France. Married Napoleon's sister Caroline, and was made King of Naples in 1808.

NELSON, HORATIO (1758-1805). British Admiral. Victor of the Battles of the Nile and Trafalgar.

NEY, MICHEL (1769-1815). Prince of Moscow, Marshal of France. He had a reputation as "The Bravest of the Brave".

PITT, WILLIAM (1759-1806). British Prime Minister during the Revolutionary and Napoleonic Wars.

SIEYÈS, EMMANUEL JOSEPH, COUNT (1748-1836). Political writer. A member of the Directory and an organiser of the *coup de Brumaire.*

TALLEYRAND-PÉRIGORD, CHARLES MAURICE DE (1754-1838). Duke of Benevento. A Bishop, a Revolutionary and Foreign Minister under Napoleon.

WELLINGTON, ARTHUR WELLESLEY, DUKE OF (1769-1852). British General, victorious in Spain and at Waterloo.

Table of Dates

1769   (15th August) Napoleon Buona Parte born in Corsica.

1785   Napoleon becomes a Lieutenant in the French Army.

1792   Fall of the French Monarchy.

1793   Napoleon commands the artillery at the Siege of Toulon.

1796   Marriage of Napoleon and Josephine Beauharnais. Napoleon commands the victorious Army of Italy and enters Milan.

1797   Napoleon captures Mantua after victories at Arcole and Rivoli.

1798   The Egyptian expedition sails. Victory of the Battle of the Pyramids. The French Fleet is destroyed at Aboukir Bay. The Second Coalition is formed in December.

1799   After the defeat at Aboukir, Napoleon leaves Egypt and sails for France. (9th-10th November) *Coup de Brumaire,* in which the Directory is overthrown and the Consulate established.

1800   The Consulate is almost unanimously approved by a plebiscite. Napoleon's victory at Marengo; Moreau defeats the Austrians at Hohenlinden.

1801   The Peace of Lunéville is agreed. Napoleon achieves the Concordat with Pope Pius VII.

1802   The Peace of Amiens is signed. Napoleon establishes the Legion of Honour. Another plebiscite supports the Life Consulship.

1803   The Peace of Amiens breaks down.

1804   The Duke d'Enghien is executed.

1805 Formation of the Third Coalition. (21st October) Battle of Trafalgar. (2nd December) Battle of Austerlitz. (26th December) Peace of Pressburg.

1807 (8th February) Battle of Eylau. (14th June) Napoleon victorious at Friedland. The Treaty of Tilsit is signed.

1808 Charles IV of Spain abdicates; Napoleon makes his brother Joseph King, and Joachim Murat King of Naples. The Spanish rise against the French, and Napoleon travels to Spain.

1809 Austria and Britain form an agreement—the Fifth Coalition. (May-July) Battles of Aspern, Essling and Wagram. The Peace of Schönbrunn is signed. Napoleon divorces Josephine.

1810 Napoleon marries Marie Louise of Austria. Holland is annexed to France.

1812 600,000 men are ready to invade Russia. (22nd July) Wellington defeats Marmont at Salamanca. (7th September) Battle of Borodino. (14th September) Napoleon enters Moscow. (25th October) the French retreat begins.

1813 Russia and Prussia join an alliance; the Sixth Coalition is formed by Britain. (21st June) Wellington is victorious at Vittoria. (18th October) Napoleon is defeated at Leipzig. France is invaded.

1814 Napoleon wages a brilliant campaign in north-east France. Paris falls to the allies; the Senate declares the deposition of Napoleon. He travels to Elba. (1st November) opening of the Congress of Vienna.

1815 Napoleon returns to France. (18th June) Battle of Waterloo. Napoleon abdicates and surrenders to the British. He is exiled to St Helena.

1821 (5th May) Napoleon Bonaparte dies on the island of St Helena.

Further Reading

A popular, easily readable biography of Napoleon is *Napoleon,* by Vincent Cronin (Collins 1971)*. The two scholarly studies of Napoleon published since the war are *Napoleon Bonaparte: his Rise and Fall,* by J. M. Thompson (Blackwell 1952) and *Napoleon,* by Felix Markham (Weidenfeld and Nicolson 1963)*. The latter is the best general study of Napoleon in English.

A very readable study of Napoleon, specializing in the military side of his genius is *Napoleon,* by David Chandler (Weidenfeld and Nicolson Great Commander series 1973).

Some interesting special studies are: *Napoleon and the Awakening of Europe,* by Felix Markham (Teach Yourself History series, English Universities Press 1954); *Europe and the French Imperium 1799-1814,* a wide-ranging study of Europe in the Napoleonic period by Geoffrey Bruun (Harper and Row 1938); *Napoleon in Russia,* by Alan Palmer (Andre Deutsch 1967); *The Letters of Napoleon,* selected, translated and edited by J. M. Thompson (Blackwell 1934); and *Napoleon: For and Against,* by P. Geyl (Cape 1964)—a very interesting study of the way historians' views of Napoleon have changed.

Some useful background books are: *Talleyrand,* by Duff Cooper (Cape 1932); *Napoleon in his Time,* by Jean Savant, trs. Katherine John (Putnam 1958)—this is a fascinating collection of extracts from the writings of Napoleon's contemporaries; *Josephine, the Empress and her Children,* by Nina Epton (Weidenfeld and Nicolson 1975)—a very warm and sympathetic study of the family side of Napoleon's life; and *The Bonapartes,* by Felix Markham (Weidenfeld and Nicolson 1975)—a very lively account of Napoleon, his brothers and sisters and what happened to their descendants.

Also available in paperback.

Index

Picture Credits

The author and publisher wish to thank those who have given permission for copyright photographs to be reproduced on the following pages: The Mansell Collection, *frontispiece,* 10, 20, 28, 29, 32 *(left),* 47, 51, 52, 56, 59, 61, 65, 66, 69, 79 *(bottom),* 81, 82, 83, 86, 89; The Mary Evans Picture Library, 44, 60, 62, 73; all other illustrations are the property of the Wayland Picture Library.

Jacket illustrations: *front,* Photographie Bulloz; *back,* the Mansell Collection.